EXPLANATION OF THE PRAYER OF THE MASS

St. Khrosrov of Andzev
Bishop of Andzev

Translated by: D.P. Curtin

EXPLANATION OF THE PRAYER OF THE MASS

Copyright @ 2023 Dalcassian Press

All rights reserved. No part of this publication may be reproduced, distributed, or transmitted in any form or by any means, including photocopying, recording, or other electronic or mechanical methods, without the prior written permission of the publisher, except in the case of brief quotations embodied in critical reviews and certain other non-commercial uses permitted by copyright law. For permission request, write to Dalcassian Press at dalcassianpublishing at gmail.com

ISBN: 979-8-3302-6172-7 (Paperback)

Library of Congress Control Number:
Author: Curtin, D.P. (1985-)

Printed by Ingram Content Group, 1 Ingram Blvd, La Vergne, Tennessee

First printing edition 2023.

EXPLANATION OF THE PRAYER OF THE MASS

EXPLANATION OF THE PRAYER OF THE MASS

EXPLANATION OF THE PRAYER OF THE MASS

According to the gospel and the Creed, the deacon is exhorted:

"And with faith let us also beseech and implore God, the Father and Almighty Lord, for it is the time of ministry and prayers, that God may make us worthy to be received."

We have said: And even more so than is usually done, let us beseech with faith. For faith makes a person acceptable, as the apostle James said: "If any of you lacks wisdom, let him ask God, who gives to all generously and without reproach, and it will be given to him. But let him ask in faith without doubting."

We are also reminded by Paul saying: "I desire that men pray in every place, lifting up holy hands, without anger and dissension." And the Lord himself confirms this to us, saying: "Whatever you ask in prayer, believe that you have received it, and it will be yours." Why does he use two words, which are: "beseech and implore?" It indicates the need for prayers to be made with great fervor and with the whole heart, to beseech with warm fervor, as the prophet advises: "Call upon the Lord, he says, and he will grant all your prayers." He attributes two names to God and even adds a third: "beseech God, the Father and Almighty Lord," reminding us to be imbued with piety towards God and to invoke with a confident spirit his mercy, providence, and help. For God is the creator, he readily comes to aid; creatures, however, require his providence. And because he is a Father through the bath of regeneration, he burns with love to have mercy on us. And because he is Almighty Lord, he undertakes to provide help and all necessary things as if to servants. Therefore, let us take refuge in him as creator and Father with steadfast love; and let us serve him as Lord with fear and turn our whole mind towards Him, and let us completely hope in Him. For if we expect to obtain all necessary things from men, to whom indeed a little mercy is due, for the sake of a single reason of fatherhood or authority, how much more should we place our highest hope in God, the Father, the Lord, to whom indeed there is much mercy? Let us repay what is owed to Him in every way. For the creature worships the Creator, and is obligated to serve and minister to Him. And a son honors the father, and a servant fears the master. If we are like this, we will be affected by all His blessings and will receive the promises of this life and the future. But if we follow those things that are contrary to these, contrary things will happen to us. And we hear this: "I regret having created man on earth," and "Behold, I will destroy them and the earth," and what He complained through the prophet: "If I am a father, where is my honor, if I am a Lord, where is my fear?"

"Because it is the hour of service and prayers, so that God may make us worthy to be received." He says this because of that hour. He indicates the time when we should be gathered for prayers. By calling it service and prayers, he shows that we should always be engaged in the service of God the Father and the almighty Lord, without laziness. And "to serve" is the name of service. He did not place service and then prayers (which mean requests) randomly, but so that you understand that it is necessary to be asked through service. For even among human masters, we are accustomed to serving first and then becoming participants in prayers. Furthermore, to make service and prayers acceptable, he advises to supplicate, i.e. to serve God as He pleases, and to pray as He desires: with holiness, love, sobriety, pure minds, fervent spirits; and to ask for beneficial things: the kingdom of God and His righteousness. As the apostle John says: "Whatever we ask according to His will, He hears us." The same applies to the following words of exhortation:

"So that the Lord may hear the voice of our supplication." May he receive the prayers of our hearts, have mercy on us. Let us serve with fear and turn our whole mind to Him and let us hope entirely in Him. For if from men, to whom indeed a little mercy is shown, we expect to obtain all necessary things for the sake of a single cause of fatherhood or power, how much more should we place our highest hope in God, the Father, the Lord, to whom indeed there is much mercy, motivated by those three [causes]? Let us repay our debts to Him in every way. For the creature worships the Creator, being obligated to serve and minister to Him. And a son honors his father, and a servant fears his master. If we are such, we will be affected by all His benefits and will receive the promises of this life and the future. But if we follow things contrary to these, contrary things will happen to us. And we hear this: "I regret having created man on earth," and "Behold, I will destroy them and the earth," and what was lamented through the prophet. If I am a father, where is my honor, if I am a master, where is my fear?

"Because it is the hour of ministry and prayers, that God may make us worthy to be accepted." For this, he says, hour. He indicates that time when we should be gathered for prayers. He calls it ministry and prayers, showing that we should always be engaged as ministers of God the Father and the Almighty Lord in His ministry, without laziness. And "to minister" is the name of service. He did not place ministry out of fear and then prayers (which signify requests), but so that you understand that it is necessary to be requested through service. For even among human masters, we are accustomed to first serve and then become participants in prayers. Furthermore, to make the ministry and prayers acceptable, he advises supplicating, i.e. that we serve God as He pleases and pray as He desires: with holiness, love, sobriety, pure minds, fervent spirits; and that we ask for useful things: the kingdom of God and His righteousness. As the apostle John says: "Whatever we ask according to His will, He hears us." The same applies to the following words of exhortation: "that the Lord may hear the voice of our supplication."

May he receive the supplications of our hearts, may he have mercy on us.

Those who usually offer such a prayer are those who ask according to his will. He then said not: "Let him receive our requests," but "our hearts," because it is not the prayers that come from the lips, but those from the heart that are accepted by him. This brings us the mercy of God, as to the harlot and the Canaanite woman, and to the blind, who did not remain silent in asking for mercy, even though many reproached them until they received sight and followed the Lord without forsaking him, not even for the sake of gifts. Let us also do this: let us not cease to pray, even if we are hindered by many obstacles, and let us not depart from him when we have received what we asked for. For he is not far from us. And we would fall into what the psalmist says: "Behold, those who are far from you will perish." But let us approach God through the admonition of the apostle, and he will also approach us.

"Our prayers and supplications shall at all times enter before his great dominion."

So let us pray as it is said; not only now, but at all times let our prayers and supplications enter before his great dominion. Then what immense joy will come to us? For if there is joy in a small dominion, as among humans, when anyone receives supplications, how much greater will be the joy when, having entered before the Lord, the Lord grants us the gifts we asked for, as if the delights of that blessedness were being offered to us, and as if we were being given them already, here, as it says: "And may he make us, working in harmony with faith in righteousness, so that the almighty Lord may bestow his mercies upon us."

You see the benefit of prayers, which is to be shown to be harmony in right faith and operation in righteousness. This happens when the almighty Lord bestows his mercy, i.e. the graces of the Holy Spirit, which the merciful one gives to those who ask. He himself is the one who rewards the works done in righteousness. He is the one who turns bitter into sweet. Afterwards, finishing with a prayer, he says:

"Revive us and have mercy on us, Lord."

Prayers

"Our Lord and Redeemer Jesus Christ, who is great in mercy and rich in the gifts of beneficence."

Although he is the Lord of heaven and earth, we call upon Him for His abundant mercy poured out; especially imploring Him as our redeemer, by whose incarnation and death we are redeemed. But if he said "great in mercy", it indicates His infinite mercy, as well as the abundance of gifts. But why does he want this to be the beginning of prayers? Because these prayers are performed at the third hour, the hour when the Redeemer was crucified, and the hour when the Holy Spirit was given to the apostles. And on the cross, out of His great mercy, He was going to suffer so that he could pay off the debts of our sins with His own body. For the same reason, those great gifts - which are: the Holy Spirit granted in abundance, with abundant and infinite beneficence. Therefore, He says, "You are great in mercy", in view of the cross; and "you are rich in gifts of beneficence", because of the outpouring of the Spirit. This is proven by the following: "Who, by your own will, endured those torments, the cross and death for our sins."

EXPLANATION OF THE PRAYER OF THE MASS

Not compelled by anyone, you willingly endured everything out of mercy for us. He does not begin speaking briefly without reason but attempts to bring many things to mind with very few words. These are: You, God and Son of God consubstantial with the Father, the creator of all, before whom the immense hosts of heaven serve with great fear, by whose command the sea is bounded by its shores and the earth is established, by whose word the stars in the firmament of heaven orbit according to their respective orders, by whose hand all kinds of living creatures are nourished, who commands all and fills all, and you are incomprehensible to all, you are inaccessible, ineffable, imperceptible: you endured sufferings, bound, brought to trial, insulted, spat upon, slapped and struck with fists, mocked, ridiculed, crowned with thorns, and burnt.

Wearing a small cloak, injured by a wooden scepter, Pilate having been scourged, now being beaten with a reed by the soldiers. By this and similar actions, he shows, saying: you have endured sufferings. Then he recounts the torments of the cross, expressing it in one word: the giving of vinegar, the affixion, the thirst, the potion of bile, the blasphemies and insults of many, and the shaking of the heads. Then he adds death to these same things, saying: By your will, you endured in that hour sufferings, the cross, and death. In this, he received a wound, even though dead. And he was even numbered among the dead in the tomb. All these things say this: "You endured for our sins," so that by your innocent blood you might free the guilty from eternal death and from torments: "and you bestowed more abundantly the gifts of your Holy Spirit on the blessed apostles." To those who mocked the apostles speaking in all languages, Peter says: "No, as you think, these are not drunk [the matter stands]. For it is the third hour of the day. The same words of prayer reveal, I say: you poured out your Holy Spirit on the blessed apostles at that same third hour when you were affixed to the cross. However, "abundantly" indicates that the apostles received more than the prophets, which is why he calls them blessed. By the eminent abundance of the Spirit, he granted them his descent. To this he adds a prayer: "Communicate to us, Lord, we beseech you, your divine gifts." "Communicating" means to share, to participate. He says "divine gift," which he attributes to the remission of sins through Christ's sufferings and the thanks he gave in the coming of the Holy Spirit. For he most clearly shows this in the following words: For having said: "Communicate to us, Lord, we beseech you, your divine gifts," he continues: "the remission of sins, the reception of your Holy

Spirit." I beseech, he says, that your precious blood, which purified the world, may also sanctify us, and that the Holy Spirit may come upon us, so that we may become partakers of their gifts and, purified from sins and filled with the Spirit, we may render thanks for your gifts in a worthy manner. This is what this [the priest] says:

"So that we may be made worthy to proclaim Father, Son, and Holy Spirit with grateful hearts; now and always and unto the ages of ages. Amen."

"Peace to all."

"Grant us your peace, Christ, our Redeemer, which surpasses all thoughts and words, keep us strong and fearless, protect us from all evil."

"This is the chapter which, according to John, was established for the possessed. For the deacons brought those possessed outside the church at that time and placed them in a part of the old temple. And while the priest offers these prayers, the whole assembly makes supplications for them."

"Grant us your peace, Christ, our Redeemer." You are the one who redeemed the human race from the slavery of Satan. And now grant redemption to them, strengthening them with your peace, which surpasses all thoughts and words. For it is not perceived by the mind or expressed in words, but it surpasses the understanding and speech of angels and humans. "Keep us strong and fearless," he says, "protect us from all evil." For it strengthens us not only against those who harass, but against all the types of demons, making us fearless with your peace."

"Unite us with those who truly worship you in spirit and truth."

For he commands those who are tormented by demons to pray apart from the assembly. For those who are deprived of the Spirit and are handed over to demons, or those who have expelled the Spirit through sins, do not have the power to unite with those who are united by the Spirit of God and who offer worship to God through this Spirit. To them the Lord himself says: "True worshipers will worship the Father in spirit and truth. For the Father seeks such worshipers for himself."

EXPLANATION OF THE PRAYER OF THE MASS

Indeed, the words of the prayers ask to be sanctified from the contamination of demons and to receive the Holy Spirit and be united with those who truly worship God in spirit and truth.

Strengthened by the Spirit in true faith and enlightened by the same, with open eyes as if in a mirror they see the glory of God and they excel in adoration before the Holy Trinity. But the prayers that are now said for all have had their words changed from ancient times. Initially, they had this meaning: Strengthen and unite those who truly adore you. But what is said now is not difficult to understand. For all calamities of sins come from that evil spirit, the demon. And it seems that those who prayed for the possessed said: Strengthen and preserve the fearless from that evil. But now we say: from all evil, that is, from all its arrows. Unite us with those who truly adore you in spirit and truth, that is: we are not worthy, but because it is just and fitting to give glory to your majesty, unite us with those who are worthy. For this is the meaning of the following words:

"For it is fitting for the most holy Trinity to have glory, principality, honor; now and always and unto the ages of ages. Amen."

In this place, as when the people are dismissed: Bless, O Lord! For now there is a speech [or assembly]. And the prayers end with blessings, and they turn to listen to the teaching and then complete the mystery. But when I have spoken elsewhere about those who are not considered suitable for listening to the sacred scriptures, I think a few things should be said here about those who say: if I hear, I do not act. Therefore, I will not listen at all, lest I incur a more severe judgment. It is necessary to say to them: O men, fearful of fear! Do you dare to say: "I do not hear or do the word of God that came from heaven"? You will only provoke God more than the Jews, because they listened when they heard. "Whatever the Lord God says to us, we will hear and do. But you never listen. If you were to dare to say from the writing of an earthly king: I do not read or hear the commands of the king,"

You would be condemned to death. The commands of God are reported, and do you despise them? Do you not think that you are guilty of eternal destruction? "Woe," says the prophet, to those who despise, by despising they despise the lawmaker." This is Isaiah. But Jeremiah, speaking in the name of the Lord: "Men of Judah and inhabitants of Jerusalem have turned their backs to me and not their faces. I taught them early, I taught, but they did not listen to receive discipline." Do you see whether God mourns more for the command not being done than for not being heard? See what Solomon says: "When distress and siege come upon you, you will call upon me, but I will not listen to you." And he says the reasons for this, before and after; before: "I called you, but you did not listen to me." I extended my words, but you did not listen, you neglected. And afterwards he says: "Evil will seek me and not find me, because they hated wisdom and did not seek the fear of God."

But the first obedience is to listen with fear to the words of God, which Isaiah commends with great benefits, saying: "Listen to the words of the Lord, you who tremble at his words." He says again: If you love me and listen, you will eat the good things of the land; but if you do not want to listen to me, the sword will eat you up. Do you see how good things are for those who listen, before they act, and how great the honor is. For through love, one turns away from evil and seeks good. And with a modest and humble mind, offer your ear to the words of God with trembling, and you will become a dwelling place of God. But who says this? God himself: "Heaven is my throne, and the earth is the footstool of my feet. And in whom will I dwell if not in the modest and humble and those who tremble at my words? And for this reason, the devil does not allow hearing, because he also knows that to those who willingly listen to the word of God, God himself gives fear and establishes his own dwelling place in them. For whom God dwells in, all difficult things become easy, laborious things become pleasant, the yoke of Christ becomes sweet, and his burden light. For the body of sin dies, and righteousness is revived, as it is written:

"If Christ is in you; then the body is dead because of sin, but the spirit lives because of justification." The apostle said this, and following it, the Lord said: "Mary has chosen the good part, which will not be taken away from her." For she was sitting at the Lord's feet and listening to his word. Consider the Lord faithful also and choose the good part that cannot be taken away. Do not believe the devil's deceit, nor deprive yourself of the good. For he wants you to become the field of his seeds. Therefore, he prevents you from receiving divine seeds. Do not believe that serpent, who deceived Eve by saying that good is not good, and enticing her with the hope of what is lacking in her. Listen to God. "Listen," he says, "with your ears, follow my ways. Hear me and you will eat good things, and your souls will rejoice in goodness." Such are the promises of life of both this one and that one! But you prefer to listen not to God but to Satan. The devil does not allow us to listen to God, so that we do not walk in God's ways and reach the good things of the Lord. He expelled us from the garden; he does not want us to live here under God's protection and, returned to God, to rejoice in immortal life. Listen to God, so that you may follow his commandments. But if you do not listen, how will you know what to do? How will you reconcile with God, not knowing by what and in what way you have provoked him? It is indeed appropriate to say to us that word of Isaiah, who says: "At that time those who seal the laws will be revealed, so that no one will be reminded and say: I will stand, I will wait for the Lord, who turns his face away from the house of Jacob, and I will hope in him." See why he does not allow the scriptures to be heard: so that those imbued with hope may not attain repentance and propitiation. If you are righteous, listen to God's commandments, and you will be strengthened in the righteousness of God. If you are a sinner, listen to God's threats and say, like David: "I have sinned against the Lord." And you will hear the same response: "The Lord has also taken away your sin." - Do not provoke God; but if you fall later, the remedy for you, who sins constantly, will be to listen constantly to God's rebukes, to say: "I have sinned," and to approach his fear: instead of rebelling, stay completely and far away from him. Remember that it is better to return to the anguish of evil.

Let him lead you, and in what matters he deceives you, and take from him as from a merciful father advice and help. It is for souls: you will recognize your wounds, and you will find remedy and health. He does not get angry when before him you fall, even if you have neglected his admonitions a thousand times, as long as [...] mode sees you approaching him and offering your wounds. He is not among the number of unskilled doctors, for he can make your invisible wounds visible. Mercy is moved by your lamenting the diseases of the soul, and immediately prepares to heal you. For he knows our frail nature, and from the abundance of various diseases he has prepared remedies: humility, confession, meekness, a forgiving attitude towards the offender, mercy, fasting, prayers, offerings, commemorations of the saints, hospitality, care for orphans and widows, compassion for brothers, so that they may be examples for us every day for the healing of souls, divine counsels advise. Above all and first of all is the perpetual sacrifice of Christ. For since we constantly fall into sin, a

EXPLANATION OF THE PRAYER OF THE MASS

sacrifice is always required for atonement. It was not enough to have sacrificed once on the cross, but he often offers the same victim for the faithful living and deceased in all the churches to God in the holy Mass. For just as he gave the world infinite atonement through the elevation of the cross, the holy Mass will give it daily. Therefore, with firm faith and great hope, we should stand before God at this hour, fearing and trembling. Abstaining from food and drink, giving alms to the poor as much as we can, confessing to God deeds contrary to the will of God, and with burning supplication we should seek atonement in the holy Mass with tears. For the most merciful God, by the death of his only begotten Son, which happened for us, will purify us from sins, free us from all guilt, and confirm and clothe us with the holy mystery, inviolate from the enemy, making us especially those who crush his head under their feet and stand unharmed by him. Therefore, the way by which minds go to God will not be obstructed, we have already enjoyed earthly goods here and are filled with hope and constant joy. However, since we have said enough about what the speech was about, we will begin to explain the words to those who are participants in the sacrament, with the help of the same one who is sacrificed [i.e. who sacrifices.].

The deacon, as the dreadful sacrament of the holy altar approaches, says: "Let no one of the catechumens, let no one of those who doubt the faith, let no one of the unrepentant approach or communicate."

Whoever is a catechumen, if present or doubting about the faith, or who has not yet undergone repentance for sins, when they leave. For when the bread and wine of the sacrifice come to the sacred altar, the heavens are opened, the heavenly descend to the earth, surrounding the altar and sanctifying it. Therefore, those who are not sanctified by baptism, not purified by penance, not believing in the faith, are expelled by this exhortation.
Explanation of the exhortation:

"Let us stand before the sacred altar of God with fear!"

This exhortation is like a call from sleep, where that altar is called the altar of God, because it stands before God and has the Son of God seated upon it. For this reason, it commands to stand before it with fear.

EXPLANATION OF THE PRAYER OF THE MASS

"Lest we be troubled by a conscience of scandal,"

It says to be troubled by a conscience of scandal: to have caused scandal through sins, which is an offense that one has not yet removed from the heart by confession, lest they stand before the sacred altar at that terrible hour.
"Lest we deceive with malice,"

Those who are called malicious fraudsters are those who pretend to have charity and peace towards their brothers and deceitfully contemplate malice in their minds. The divine mystery does not admit them, but expels them.

"not cunningly devising deceit," The cunning are full of deceit, towards God and towards men: especially those who present themselves as orthodox in faith, when they are heterodox; or pretend to be just, when they are sinners; or appear before men as something they are not in reality: honest or sincere; and any other deceit, falsehood, deception, by which one displays in oneself what is not there. The Lord excludes them saying: "Depart from me, all you who work iniquity."

"not doubting with imperfect faith," They doubt with imperfect faith who pronounce the faith, which we profess according to the holy Gospel, to be in some way doubtful and imperfect; or those who do not believe in this holy sacrament as the flesh and blood of God; or those who in any way lack hope in him [i.e. they have little hope.]. These must first be corrected by prayers and admonitions of the scriptures, as it is written: "He must first be purified, and then approach the pure."

"but with just morals," Just morals are those required by law: not perverse to the right or left.

"with sincere hearts," That is: manifesting what they are, not pretending.

"with harmonious minds," Simple towards God and men, with thoughts nowhere twisted.

"with perfect faith," This is the perfection of faith: to know the Father and the Son and the Holy Spirit, three persons and one God, not professing about them "more" or "less", "first" or "later", but plainly equal and of the same nature.

The Father is the Generator, the Son is the Begotten, and the Spirit proceeds. Born of the eternal three, and from the beginning with the Father the Son and the Holy Spirit. The Son became incarnate from Mary, ineffably, without change. The same truly God and perfect man. Manifesting the power of divinity as God and bearing human sins as a man, of one nature. The same one underwent the cross and death and rose on the third day, and removed our curse, sins, and death. Clothed in our flesh, he ascended into heaven and will come to judge the living and the dead, and to render to each according to their works: to the righteous, eternal life, and to the sinners, eternal torment. Also, confess baptism as the second birth in the Holy Spirit into the adoption of the heavenly Father. Then believe in this saving sacrament as the true flesh and blood of Christ, by which we are united with Christ and become his heirs. If these are believed, faith is perfect.

"full of love," full of the love of God and not lacking in brotherly love.

"abounding in all good works," i.e. those that proceed from the love of God and brethren, are good.

"let us approach the sacred altar of God," It reminds us to approach the altar of God again, so that the sermon may end with even greater reverence. "and we shall find mercy on that day when the second coming of our Redeemer will appear." It recalls the terrible advent of Christ, so that we do not approach untested to the divine table. For if we approach agitated in conscience, we are greatly reproved, like the one who entered the wedding feast in filthy garments. But when we have cleansed the filth and put on the wedding garments, as we are reminded by the exhortation, we will obtain mercy on that day and enjoy the blessings of Christ through his mercy. For even if we were imbued with six hundred labors of righteousness, the gifts are still by mercy, and indeed much more than the fruit of our labor. He concludes the exhortation with prayers, saying: "Almighty Lord our God, revive us and have mercy on us."

For unless we are helped by Your mercy, we cannot acquire that purity which would allow us to be united with You. By Your mercy we shall become worthy and shall receive eternal life.

EXPLANATION OF THE PRAYER OF THE MASS

Prayers of the Priest

"Lord God of hosts and creator of all that exists," We have often said in other supplications that the name of the Lord comes from ruling. "God," however, comes from creating and bringing into existence the things in the world. "Of hosts," that is, of angels, because not only the earth and all that is in it belong to God as their Lord, but also the heavens and the heavenly beings, as the prophet says: "Bless the Lord, all you His angels, you mighty in strength, who do His word."

"And creator of all that exists," that is, whatever exists is established by Your command. But those who say this and those who deserve to hear it should know that in the presence of God stands one who has spiritual and angelic powers as his ministers, who spoke to all things, and they were made, commanded, and confirmed.

"Who from nothing brings all things into being created." "From nothing" means: from non-existence; "bringing all things" means all things; "into being" into appearance and sight; "created" you made things exist that were not, you made insubstantial things substantial, you made substances that were not into essences, you called into sight things that did not exist. These words are few, they have a hidden meaning. Not were the heavens and the heavens of the heavens. Not the various and innumerable hosts of the heavens, not the sun, not the moon, not the stars, not the air, not the clouds, not the rain, not the earth, not the fire, not the springs, rivers, seas. Not the various species of plants and herbs and seeds, each having its own smell and flowers and fruits and tastes. Not the diverse animals and beasts and reptiles and birds and fish. Not the precious and useful materials: gold, silver, gems, iron, copper, lead, glass, and the like. Not the sources of oil or those which produce salts from waters and mountains, but these and whatever else exists, brought forth from nothing.

By the will of God, things were suddenly done and became visible. And therefore, from this thanksgiving began, so that throughout the whole holy Mass we may give thanks, and tremble, stand before the almighty and all-creating Lord with great fear, and offer our prayers and approach the holy mystery with all holiness. "Who, most lovingly honoring our earthly human nature, ordained for the ministry of such ineffable and terrible sacrament,"

"He calls human nature 'earthly' because the body was created from the earth. He calls the priesthood 'honor' and says: 'most lovingly honoring the human race,' because God loved humans and gave them honor even above the angels. He says 'ineffable and terrible' holy sacrifice. 'Ineffable' because it is not expressed in words what it is, and 'terrible' because of the awe-inspiring glory. For those who have seen it, whether from the incorporeal angels or the corporeal saints, it was intolerable and fearful. But no one has seen all of its greatness. For no one has ever seen God. Therefore, if the Son of God became flesh, God is invisible to all earthly nature and to the minister [i.e. not even in Christ is the divine nature seen with the eyes]. He spoke above of the greatness of God in the dominion of heavenly powers, then in creation, and now here: in ineffable and terrible honor. And because you are so great, out of the love of your kindness you have raised dust to such honor, that the minister of the ineffable mystery may be. We say this to Christ as we offer Him as a sacrifice to the Father. Therefore, it continues: 'You, Lord, to whom we offer this sacrifice, accept this offering from us.'"

"'Sacrifice' is what is offered. 'You, Lord,' we say to the Father, to whom we humans offer such a victim, which the priest's prayer called 'sacrifice.' And you, he says, are accustomed to receive: now also accept what we have proposed. In every sacrifice, in order for the celebrant to be worthy, it is first asked. Here also, prayer has this understanding."

May God not consider it as something contemptible when we celebrate. This is what he says: "Accept from us." Just as you have honored our nature.

And you allow men to offer such a sacrifice to you, that you may clearly present yourself to us, making visible the things we have transgressed. Let us be conscious of the whole, but especially of the terrible mystery at the time of our transgressions, and let the perversities be recalled by us in memory. And remembering the errors, let us cast away all arrogance, considering the worthlessness of our nature. For if Abraham the patriarch, in whose conscience no fault was found, but who held God as witness to his great righteousness, nevertheless, when speaking there, professed that he was not only dust, but also ashes, how much more should our sinful nature and harmful disposition be humbled? For a humble spirit is a sacrifice to God, and especially approaches God, who humbles and purifies the soul from the consciousness of evils; for God does not despise a holy soul and a humble spirit. And accomplish this for the sacrament of your only begotten Son's body and blood, "Perfection" we usually call the consummation of things. We say that this is consummated if it is the flesh and blood of the Son of God. What follows is the mystery of God, revealed by Himself; and He reveals this to His saints; it is a secret to the defiled, lest holiness be given to dogs, and lest a gem be cast before swine, lest it be trampled underfoot. Therefore, let us not give such a sacrament to unbelievers in case we are mocked by them, i.e. lest our souls be affected by bitterness. For the word of the cross is foolishness to the perishing. Not in vain has the term "only begotten" been used instead of "son," but so that we may be reminded that we have found such great love of God, that He sacrificed His only Son, who was begotten by Him, for us.

"As we partake of this remedy for the forgiveness of sins, grant us this bread and wine, through the grace and love of our Lord and Redeemer Jesus Christ," By partaking, we have sinned and become mortal, so that we may acquire expiation and immortality by partaking of the sufferings of Christ. I pray over this bread and wine placed on the altar, that they may become the body and blood of Christ for expiation.

Let us give life to the living and the dead. And this because of the love of Christ, who died for us, which he calls grace and charity. For no one is without sin, and there are many things that we have sinned about in ignorance. But those who confess and repent receive expiation through this holy sacrament and are once again united with Christ, so that they may be his body and members. Therefore, we seek this great medicine.

"With you, Almighty Father, together with the life-giving and liberating Holy Spirit, befitting glory, dominion, honor."

He calls the Father Almighty because by his power he holds the heavens and the earth and all that they contain. He called the Holy Spirit life-giving and liberating, because through him baptism has regenerated us to become children of God, freeing us from sins and giving us life to immortal life. He also accomplishes this holy sacrament, giving us life and liberation.

He also gives us a future renewal in the resurrection. Therefore, it is right and worthy to glorify the most holy Trinity with these words: "befitting glory, dominion, honor"; "now and forever and unto ages of ages."

Exhortation

"Greet one another with a kiss of holiness!"

The kiss of holiness is made holy by a holy love, not by malicious or impure counsel, but with a simple attitude towards one's brother.

"If you cannot partake, instruct one another and pray at the gates!"

"Christ is offered as a sacrifice."

Because Christ is the one who is sacrificed, let those whose souls are unclean and defiled depart, for those who enjoy spiritual joy are unworthy. Let them teach each other the sacred scripture and pray at the gates. Let them deplore injustices with a contrite heart and burning tears, for they have been expelled from the spiritual wedding feast, as they are not worthy at that terrible hour to approach the heavenly table or to sing with the angels gathered here or to be united with Christ in the holy sacrament and to be of one spirit with him. But those who, while this sacrament is being celebrated, depart, confessing their sins with fear and prayer before God, will quickly obtain reconciliation through Christ's sacrifice and will obtain expiation. But those who are slow have departed from the sight of God and have distanced themselves from the holy ones do not prepare themselves for repentance, but considering this daily, they leave happily and remain careless, they even more provoke the gentle anger of God. For they do not bear to be punished and separated from the holy ones and removed from Him [i.e. God], therefore they are certainly judged. Let us fear, let us be fearful and let us pay close attention!"

For if the bodiless hosts, although holy in all things, stand from the beginning up to this point in timid fear before the glory of God, how much more should we who are always entangled in sins tremble and be horrified? And what does it mean to pay close attention? Not to pay attention as those who remain inside advise them to mere bread and

EXPLANATION OF THE PRAYER OF THE MASS

wine, but to believe that the body and blood of God are present before us, and to stand with great fear and as if observing God. This chapter follows, which teaches: "Christ is offered as a sacrifice before us, the Lamb of God," This is the reason for which we are commanded to fear and tremble. For he who assumed flesh from the virginal womb of Mary and was united with her [i.e. flesh] through the power of his entire divinity, is now united in the same way with the bread and the cup. And he who expired on the cross, bearing the likeness of one expiring and showing on the altar this same death according to the flesh, is offered as a living victim by his divinity as a sacrifice to the holy Trinity: thanksgiving for the gifts we have received, expiation for the sins we have committed, liberation from future sins, intercessor of the living and the dead for eternity. This is what ancient rites of sacrificing animals signified: some sacrifices were for the sake of thanksgiving, others for expiation, others for the sake of redemption; all of which are encompassed in this great sacrifice. Before this chapter, where we are commanded to pay close attention, those who are present say: "To you, O God," that is, we look at you and believe that you change these offerings into the incorruptibility of your divinity. But for this chapter they say: "mercy and peace and the sacrifice of blessing!"

The protester manifests in his words what we have already said. For mercy is, insofar as it is an expiation of sins. Peace is, insofar as it grants redemption to souls and bodies and peace. For some of the ancient sacrifices were also called pacifying. Finally, the sacrifice is a blessing, because it is offered to God in thanksgiving for all His benefits, which have befallen us from the beginning until now. We bless God throughout this whole sacrifice, as the words of the celebrants [i.e., clerics] indicate: "May the grace, love, and divine power that sanctifies the Father, the Son, and the Holy Spirit be with all of you." This is what Paul wrote to the Corinthians: "May the grace of our Lord Jesus Christ, the love of God, and the communion of the Holy Spirit be with all of you." And the one who celebrates the sacrifice gives these to the assembly: that whatever has been expiated through the incarnation of Christ and gifts have been given, and the love of God the Father, who has adopted believers, and the communion of the Spirit which is holy, be with you. For having been reconciled and united in the love of God, and partakers of the Holy Spirit in the heavenly bridal chamber with the immortal bridegroom, we shall be.

EXPLANATION OF THE PRAYER OF THE MASS

Then those who are nearby say - not as when peace is given in prayer, for there they say: "and with your spirit," but here it is "from your spirit." For just as the spirit of Moses was given to seventy-two elders, so indeed from your spirit [i.e., the priest's] may it be given to us, who, like Moses, have approached God and offer our thanksgivings and prayers. "Lift up your hearts in this divine mystery!" For although the sacrifice is performed here on earth, it is heavenly. Therefore, that divine Paul writes: "Set your minds on things above, not on things that are on earth."

And the response is: "We lift them up to you, Almighty Lord." i.e. to you, Almighty Lord, we lift up our minds, so that the soul may dwell there and direct the whole body from there. "And give thanks to the Lord with your whole mind!" Wanting to begin the thanksgivings, he admonishes all.

To lift up the whole mind according to the words of thanksgiving and to give thanks to God. They say: "Worthy and just." He is worthy to whom thanks are given, and it is just to give thanks for his benefits, because we owe this.

Explanation of the prayers that the priest secretly says.

"Truly it is worthy and just, with the most prompt diligence to adore and glorify you, who were and are and will be, the eternal and unfathomable God, the Trinity of three persons in one unity, always adoring by glorifying."

According to what the assembly said, the priest repeats: "truly it is worthy and just." Indeed, he says, it is just. "Most prompt diligence": diligence means to care with the whole mind. However, most prompt diligence indicates the utmost ardor of the soul, which is ready with the whole mind and operation and thought for diligence, according to Paul's admonition: "In diligence, do not be lazy in spirit!" Therefore, it is worthy to be lifted up to adore you who were and are and will be God, who existed before eternities and now are and remain in the eternities of eternities. "Eternal": you have no beginning or end in essence. And "unfathomable": neither angels nor humans scrutinize, what kind you are, or find out.

"Trinity of three persons in one unity" three persons and one nature, which is deity. It is worthy, he says, to adore with the most prompt

EXPLANATION OF THE PRAYER OF THE MASS

diligence the eternal, unfathomable Trinity, always glorifying. And why it should be glorified and adored with such diligence, he says, turning to the Father: "who through your, Father, insensible and creating Word, removed the obstacle of curses."

He calls the Word the Son. For he was born immaculately from the Father, just as a word is born from the mind. And he reveals the will of the Father, as the word reveals the will of the speaker. And just as the word is carried to many through one voice, undivided [so is the Son]. And he was incarnated, seemed, touched, who was like the incorporeal word, which is embodied in paper, becoming visible and tangible. And he is inseparable from the Father, as the word is spread to others sounding and at the same time remains in the mind. He is called "insensible" because the nature of God is incomprehensible and intangible. "Creating" because creation is common to the Trinity. And because by deceit a curse was placed as an obstacle between us and God, that is, an obstacle placed between us separated us from God and from the garden and from life; God, having mercy on us, removed what was an impediment from the curse. Neither an angel nor a holy person was commanded to do this, but the co-creating Son. Through the Son, therefore, he removed, who as his own people appropriated from the church those who believe in you. Within the church, those who believe in you, he made his own people. "His own" means: stable and not opposing. He established us, saying, a people clinging to him, inseparable from his dominion. And he deigned to dwell in us according to his sensible nature through his incarnation from the Virgin. John the evangelist says this: "The Word became flesh and dwelt among us." This is what you say: because the Word is insensible, as was said a little while ago, it took flesh from the Virgin and became sensible. Just as John writes in the Catholic epistle: "Our hands have touched the word of life..." The incarnation is the undertaking of the work. For the Son of God undertook this work in himself, so that he might become the son of man from the Virgin. To dwell in us is to be like us. What the prophet Isaiah says about the son of the virgin: "They shall call his name Emmanuel," which means: God with us. "And he worked a new work, as God; he transformed the earth into heaven." Indeed, he worked a new work when he transformed the earth into heaven, which is possible only by the artifice of God. For he who created the earth from nothing at first, now made heaven from the earth. And how this was done, he says in these words: "For before whom the hosts of the vigilant [i.e. angels] could not stand, they trembled at the dazzling and The terrible light of divinity, that is, to whom such greatness belongs, became man for our redemption, granting us to leap with the celestial beings at least spiritual leaps."

Have you seen how the earth has ascended to heaven? The Lord of heavens and angels descended to earth, became man, made humans angels. And he gathered together the heavenly hosts and humans into one. And he allowed their songs to be sung on earth along with those of the earthly beings.
Before we bring this most beautiful chapter to an end, it is necessary to contemplate the admirable harmony of it, I say, how the magnitude of divine grace ascending from one thing to another is excellently described [by the priest].

Therefore, see as you go through from the beginning: It is truly worthy and just, with all diligence, for you who were, are, and will be, to adore and glorify eternal and unfathomable God, the Trinity, who through your, Father, removed the obstacle of the insensible and creating Word of curses. It was a great gift to be liberated from curses. But greater is what the only begotten Son did, who himself escaped the curse and gave us the blessing. Not content with this, he also appropriated us as his people, who were under a curse. This is much higher than being freed from curses. Furthermore, another gradation: he became, like us, and dwelt among us, which is much more sublime than because we have become his people. And what is even greater is that he made the earth heaven, and humans angels. These things infinitely surpass that which he, whom the angels serve with great fear, granted us to sing fearlessly with them the songs of angels, which they sing with great fear, and, as if we were gentiles and their kinsmen through love, to take their ministry upon ourselves.

Therefore, let us contemplate the remaining words individually: For they could not endure to stand before the joyful hosts. The heavenly beings are called joyful because they are always imbued with joy and happiness seeing God and his most merciful. Arranged among themselves, they carry out the ministry of God, divided into various choirs, which prayer has called "ranks." And if he said they could not stand before him, he said this because Isaiah and Ezekiel the prophet, one of the Seraphim, the other of the Cherubim, as far as they could, described to us trembling with much fear. For Ezekiel reports that the wings of the Cherubim were extended over the head and the whole body, as if in great fear they covered themselves with their wings, he says. Isaiah, on the other hand, describes the wings of the Seraphim, which were also six, as being divided into two parts, covering two faces, two feet from the divine fire, always in motion from the force of terrible visions. Emulating each other and shouting with a dreadful noise among themselves. Therefore, he says: "They could not stand before him," that is, they could not. Trembling at the flashing and terrible light of divinity." For the terrible light of the divine majesty pours forth intolerable thunderbolts and immediately afflicts them with horror, trembling, and consternation. "He who is of such greatness became man for our redemption," that is, whose glory was so terrible and intolerable, he, in order to redeem us, became man, descended to our poverty, and bestowed his divinity upon us. But he does not mention this, but that which made him a companion of angels: "He granted us," he says, "to dance spiritual dances with the heavenly beings." "Dancing" indicates: to be of the same choir. He speaks of heavenly and spiritual dances of those who are companions of the heavenly and spiritual beings. He did this by grace, not according to merit, that is, forgiving, pitying, and pardoning. For this is what he means by saying, "granted." "So that by singing with the Seraphim and Cherubim, we may modulate the canticles of the Trisagion," "Canticle is the name of the song... Singing:" the same as to sing which they do. "Trisagion": to say the same Trisagion blessing that the Seraphim sing. And "to modulate": to adapt to their modulation. "So that with confidence rejoicing together with them, we may jubilate and say": "The Lord of glory has become our brother, even more than the Seraphim, with them we shout this Trisagion: Holy, holy, holy, Lord God of hosts." It is shouted thrice: according to the three persons: the Father and the Son, and the Holy Spirit. And one Lord: because one of the three dominion is divine. Lord of hosts", that is, of angels, because they are strong in power and because they are the forces of the king of heaven. The heavens and the earth are full of your glory." The heavens through the heavenly ones, and the earth through the earthly ones, lift up your praises; not only through speaking and thinking animals, but through all creatures, which by their very existence proclaim the glory of God. "Blessed in the highest," the Father, whom we call the heavenly Father. Although he is not only in the highest, but everywhere, we still say that he is there, because those who are there do his will in all things. Blessed is he who came and will come in the name of the Lord." He speaks of the Son, who came to liberate creatures and will come to judge the human race. "In the name of the Lord": because in the name of his Father he came, as he himself said: "I come in the name of my Father." Likewise, he called himself Lord; and he is the Lord. "Blessed in the highest," that is, in the heavens: to the Holy Spirit, whose coming from heaven upon the Lord in the Jordan and upon the apostles in the upper room [was indicated] by these words.

But if we say "blessed in the highest", to the Father and to the Holy Spirit, so we say to the Redeemer humbling himself to us, we intend to proclaim him with the attitude of imitating the children in their shouting. Just as they, seeing him seated on a young donkey, said using the Davidic word: "blessed is he who comes in the name of the Lord," so we also, seeing him on the holy altar through his precious body and blood, bless him. "Truly" signifies "truly," and "all holy": in all things holy. And "holy" signifies: glorified. For one who possesses glory without any defect is truly glorified, and completely glorified. Among us, one who is pure is called holy.

But our venerable teachers, in this hymn, taught that what the angels say signifies "glorified." "And who can grasp with words your infinite outpourings of mercy towards us?"

"No one," he said, "can grasp and express in words, that is: all that your mercy has poured out upon us, no one can fully express, because they are infinite and incomprehensible. To show mercy is more than to have compassion. Parents bestow this with burning love upon their children with great compassion. This can be seen not only in humans, but often in other animals as well, as the Lord likened himself and Jerusalem to a hen. Therefore, he gives thanks for the immense outpouring upon us, because not only should we give thanks when they are abundant, but especially when he has increased his blessings out of burning love, great mercy, and soothing inexplicable mercy. And because our nature was poor and had nothing to offer as a gift before God and had not given thanks for the benefits placed before God, therefore God did not want us to be expiators, but prepared to give us his only begotten son with immeasurable and infinite love, so that through him we may be powerful and lay him down before God and give thanks for the good things that have happened to us through him. Therefore, offering the sacrifice on the altar, we begin to give thanks from the very beginning. But first, the prayer confesses that there is no

EXPLANATION OF THE PRAYER OF THE MASS

ability to express in words all the benefits bestowed upon us. And then the thanksgiving begins:

"You immediately lifted up the fallen into sins from the beginning through various modes of care,"

First, this means that from the beginning, you consoled the human race fallen into sins through various cares. "To lift up" means to console, and "multiple" signifies diverse: "Through modes" means through changes. Sometimes, the long life of good and upright fathers has taught their children the ways of justice. It happens that some have been honored with grace, like Enoch through translation. And sometimes, it happened that transgressors were punished, like Cain and those who lived during the time of the flood, and the Sodomites. For this too is the providence of God, to punish."

And he shall cut off sins and make others cautious. He made a covenant again with the righteous and redeemed them, like Noah, Abraham, and his offspring, like Lot, Jacob, who were all righteous, and their sons - Israel, whom he freed from Egypt, he kept in the desert, to whom he gave laws, among whom he raised prophets, to whom he gave the land of promise, priesthood, and kingdom, he gave victims, offerings, and sacrifices. For they were to receive, until the truth would come, through the shadow of truth, consolation. Moreover, he spoke through angels and appeared in various forms as God himself. And for the number of nations, he appointed from his angels [i.e. guardians]. He indicated these and many other similar things, saying: "You have been relieved through multiple ways of care": through prophets, the donation of laws, priesthood, sacrifices, which was like a shadow offering."

For all the offerings of ancient times were either for the sake of sins or redemption or praise.

They prefigured Christ sacrificing. And the burnt calves, with whose ashes they were sprinkled, contaminated, showed our purifications that are made through Christ's washing and sacrifice. Therefore, the apostle says: "The laws had a shadow of future goods, not the very image of things." A shadow is what we call opaque and what is made by a body, whether of an animal or any other thing. And he calls present things future goods, which were prepared for us through

Christ, so that they might happen to us at this hour, which Paul also says more clearly in another epistle. He gave figures that are shadows of the future, but Christ is the body." Therefore, learn that the shadow of the laws was made by Christ, who transformed the figures. And know how much space there is between the shadow [i.e. how much space the shadow occupies]. The one from whom the shadow is made, how great he is, so great is the interval between the laws and grace given to us.

"And by taking away the judgment of all our sins at the end of these days."

He says: "the end of days," because in the six days of creation, six millennia of this life are indicated; and on the seventh, the future life begins. Therefore, since in the last millennium, which is the sixth, the grace of God was manifested through Christ, there is no complete millennium age after this. Therefore, he calls it "the end of days".

A space of a thousand years, understanding the final millennium. Paul also explained this by saying: "At the end of these days he spoke to us through the Son".

"Removing the judgment of all our debts, indeed. 'Omnium' means 'all.' 'Debita' refers to transgressions. The Lord also taught us to pray for this: 'Forgive us our debts.' Judgment is said to be that which kings write about the guilty and seal up, until they pay according to their transgressions. Likewise, the human race from the first man to Christ is as if written and sealed, awaiting the day of judgment for rebellions of thoughts, words, and deeds, which is removed through the judgment by Christ. Let us return to the prayer: 'And at the end of these days, removing the judgment of all our debts,'

'You gave us your only begotten as debtor and debts,'

You removed, he says, the judgment, not by force, but by right, so that your just sentence may not fail. You appointed your only begotten as the one to be guilty of our sins, not from among angels or saints, but your only begotten. Recalling the abundant love, he gives thanks again: you begot the one, you gave him to us as debtor, who not by anyone else, but by himself, paid for our sins. The Lord," says David, "repaid on my behalf." And 'debts,' according to Isaiah: "He was delivered, he says, for our sins." And the Lord himself: "So," he says, "God loved the world that he gave his only begotten son." And Paul: He did not spare his own son, but gave him up for us all. "Your only begotten," he says, "you gave us as debtor and debts,"

"victim and anointed one, lamb and heavenly bread, high priest and sacrifice."

Not only did you give your only begotten as debtor and debts, he says, but as victim and anointed one, because in place of the united priests you gave him, that he may be anointed and high priest for us, victim and lamb of sacrifice and bread of offering. For according to certain laws, in the morning and evening, the priests offered daily lambs, and placed on the table the bread of offering that was to be there each day. Each offered the sacrifices of their assemblies. And with the blood of animals, they announced the purity of bodies."

Your true only-begotten Son, who is the same for all of us, purifies not only the contamination of the body, but purifies the soul and the whole body, not in the likeness of a figure and shadow, but in truth. Just as he himself said: "For their sakes I sanctify myself," so that they themselves may also be sanctified in truth." Saying: "in truth" the ancient sanctifiers indicated that they were figures, not truly sanctifiers.

Therefore, speaking: "You have given us your only begotten debtor and debts, victim and anointed one" indeed who sacrifices the victim the lamb and the heavenly bread, the high priest and the sacrifice", he adds here:

"Because he is the distributor, and he himself is distributed among us perpetually and inexhaustibly."

Paul often repeats all these things: Christ was the high priest; he offered the sacrifice; with his own blood, he entered into eternal sanctification; we have an altar, from which it is not allowed to taste for those who serve in the ministry of the tabernacle. In this table, Christ is the distributor, and he is the one who is distributed. Just as in the upper room he distributed to the apostles and was distributed, so from that day until now to all the faithful in all the churches he himself distributes and is distributed and is not consumed.

Therefore he says: he is distributed in us, inexhaustible. Then, with such great grace manifested and described, he shows why the high priest and the sacrifice and the anointed one and the heavenly bread and the distributor and the distribution are; with these words: "Because he truly became man and not in appearance." Not in appearance, he says, i.e. not in pretense, but truly became man, "and incarnated in a united union from the holy and divine virgin Mary," He says, united with flesh in a mingled manner. For he did not change or destroy the divine nature or the human, but united the natures, and so he is the same God and the same man, so that the divine word is man, and he who was incarnated from the virgin is God; and the same God is also man; and Mary, who gave birth to the divine word, is the divine mother and virgin.

"He underwent all the conditions of human life except sins"

Scriptures usually call life a journey, which Christ passed through all the conditions of the flesh without truly
sinning. That is: he was born, he was nurtured, he hungered, he thirsted, he was weary he ate, he drank, he was clothed, he was concerned, he was troubled, he was saddened, he wept, and all other things that are borne in the body, he accepted. The word overcame the faults of men's remaining sins and of his own accord ascended the saving cross, the cause of our redemption."

And the Lord demonstrated that the crucifixion is the cause of the life of the world and the redemption of humanity. Therefore, giving thanks in prayer calls the saving cross the cause of our redemption.

"He took the bread into his most holy, life-giving hands," and it was given.

Truly divine were those most holy hands; and 'life-giving,' in that they gave life to humanity in creation. And through the same hand that was new life, there is now newness. For it is the same hand that created Adam:
incorporeal then, now corporeal. That which transformed dust into a human endowed with reason and speech, that same almighty and life-

giving hand transformed the bread received into the divine body. He united there [with the body] the human soul, united here the divine nature.

There, it is said in scripture, he breathes into the face the spirit, which is the Holy Spirit, creating in man the vital soul. And here it says in scripture: He took the bread and blessed it. And to bless is to introduce the Holy Spirit. Sent to Mary. He accomplished the ineffable incarnation in her and united with the divine Word the flesh, which was from a virgin, he will also make the bread a miracle united with the Son of God.

"He blessed," it says, he gave thanks,"

Our high priest offered his body as a sacrifice, as one of the men gives thanks to God for the benefits that befall our race from the beginning forever. And he gave this gift in satisfaction on behalf of mankind.

Then he says: "He gave to his chosen disciples saying: Take, eat all of this; this is my body, which is distributed for you and for many." There were other disciples of the Lord, but the first place was held by the twelve whose prayer called them the chosen ones. He gave this holy sacrament to the first ones. Because He was about to give the bread to the faithful, he mentions next the distribution, which would be made to many, showing what inexhaustible food he would truly give to the faithful from that day until the end of the world.

"In the same way, he took the cup, blessed it, gave thanks, and gave it to his chosen disciples: Take, drink from this all of you: this is my blood of the new testament, which is shed for you and for many for the forgiveness of sins."

Beginning our sacrifice, the Lord taught that it should be completed with thanksgiving. For we give thanks not only for creation, but also for the care and redemption of all people. Let us continue with a grateful memory through the holy sacrifice for all the benefits that have come to everyone and to each individually. For the Lord came not only to redeem and save us, but also to be a teacher for all orders and laws. Therefore, take note from the very beginning: He was born, he chose a poor mother, so that you may not consider poverty, which the king of all loved, as something to be avoided. The child was driven out to Egypt and often, when he had bestowed benefits with miracles, he was driven out so that you may not abhor persecutions or be indignant if those to whom you have granted benefits also trouble you. For you can never bestow such great benefits as he, who indeed was God and redeemer. Also, consider that you are not as free from sins as he, who was entirely immaculate. Nor can you think yourself more worthy of honor and distinctions than the Son of God. He wore clothes not for the sake of adornment, but to cover his body, so that you may use what is necessary, not what is superfluous. He ate and drank as he was dressed, not giving himself over to luxury, but using things moderately that are necessary for life. He attended weddings and showed a modest appearance of cheerfulness, giving a wonderful gift. He showed the measure of tears and mourning grieving for the beloved Lazarus.

He also gave an example to travelers on how to relieve the burden of work for animals. For he did not ride on a golden donkey or horse. The rein was tightened. He also taught how one should pray in temptations, and what kind of gentleness should be shown towards tempters, and that good should be repaid for evil, just as he himself healed the ear of the servant. Therefore, just as in all other aspects of his life, especially in the most diverse humiliations, he also wanted to teach us by washing the feet of the disciples, how the mystery should be accomplished: with a blessing, I say, and thanksgiving, he taught. And because he wants to be a debtor to us himself and not us to him, therefore, if we give thanks to God, he rewards us with the same great sacrifice. For the debts of the dead and the living will be paid through him, and the same God will be both creditor and debtor. Therefore, giving the cup to the disciples, he said: "This is my blood of the new testament, which is shed for you and for many for the remission of sins." He indicated the blood that was to flow from the cross, and the piercing of the nails and the splitting of the side. He called it blood not only his own blood, but he called it the new testament. For in the old testament, which was made with the Jews concerning the land of promise, the blood was of animals; but in this new testament, it is his precious blood.

Therefore, God predicted through Jeremiah, that he would make a new covenant, putting his laws in our minds and thoughts, becoming our God, making his people us, not remembering our sins and wickedness. He not only said that he would make a pact with his blood, but he also added this: We make a pact with you, me and the Father, about the kingdom, and about you being joyful with me. For he indicated our joy with him by saying: "Eat and drink at my table in the kingdom of my Father." "So that we may always do this in his memory, the kind and loving Lord of men commanded us." For the Life-Giver said: Whenever you eat this bread and drink this cup, you proclaim my death until I come. For this reason, we say that he commanded us to do what he himself accomplished, to perform the sacrifice in memory of his death. It is always: perpetual. "And he descended into the lower place of death." "Lower" means inner place. Thus, he calls that tomb, the divine body that he had taken from Mary was placed. For he says, "And he descended into the lower regions of death" with his body that he had received from our consanguinity.

He calls the Virgin Mary, his own mother, consanguineous and holy. And just as his body descended into the tomb in likeness to other bodies, so his soul came to other dead souls and gave great exaltation to the saints and broke the strength of death. Therefore, he adds here: "and breaking strongly the bars of the underworld, he surely showed himself to be the God of the living and the dead."

Namely, so that the return to bodies is open to souls imprisoned, and there is resurrection for bodies. For the Lord had threatened Adam with death if he ate of the fruit. But the transgressor of the law, because he was found, was subjected to death and sins with his offspring. No one among men was found who could pay the debt of death with their innocence. The son of Adam became the Son of God, innocent of sins, and died for sinners and debtors. Afterwards, he overcame death by breaking its gates and rescuing its captives. He could have done this even without his own death, as he did with Lazarus. And he did not want to redeem by power alone, but also by justice. Like one of the prophets said: "His captivity will be redeemed by justice and mercy." "Mercy": because he became man, and died for us. And "justice": because the death of the innocent will vindicate life for the guilty. He placed before our eyes the closed prison, whose gates he says are broken, to show as if chains, whose gates are broken and barriers are shaken; as he said: "breaking". And especially a tyrant, when held in unbreakable chains, is no longer an obstacle to escape. From this likeness, resurrection will not happen by our own virtue, because Christ has overcome death. And from all this, it is known for sure, that is truly known, that he who died is the God of the living and the dead. Just as the apostle says: "Christ died and lived, so that he may rule over the dead and the living."

And therefore, we, O Lord, according to that command, offer this life-giving sacrament of the body and blood of your only begotten Son. Because he ordered, he said, that what he himself did, we should do the same. This is what he means by that: according to this commandment we offer". To offer is: to place on the altar bread and wine, which is the sacrament of the body and blood of the Son of God. This is a sacrament, because it must be believed not by seeing, but by knowing. For bread and wine appear, but the body and blood of the Son of God are known. And it is called salutary", because we are saved by it and we are saved, in life and in death.

"We commemorate his saving sufferings for us," Therefore, saying: we commemorate what he himself suffered for us, let us consider in our minds that the Son of God was bound in order to free us from the bonds of sins; that he was condemned by the impure, in order to render us uncondemned judging the earth; that his divine face was violated by spittle and his cheeks by slaps, in order to renew his image deformed by us; that his holy head was struck by fists, veiled by a purple cloak, in order to remove the veil of darkness from our minds and the various torments of soul disturbances, that he was affected by mockery with a crown of thorns, a reed, a jesting adoration, in order to truly make us kings and deify us, to give us the garment of honor, the diadem of the kingdom, the scepter of power; that he was affected by ignominy when he was mocked by Herod, scourged by Pilate, in order to make us glorious and prepare for us an indolent life in eternity.

"life-giving crucifixion," Because we were dead in sins, he died on the cross and turned our death into life. Therefore we call his ascension to the cross life-giving.

"three-day incorruptible burial," For according to the prophet his soul was not abandoned in hell, nor did his flesh see corruption, but he also rescued our souls from hell and freed our flesh from corruption.

"blessed resurrection," Blessed in the scriptures means: filled with all good. He who is truly blessed is like God himself, who is not only the Blessed One, but also the giver of all blessedness. For when he became man and flesh, the resurrection demonstrated him as God.

EXPLANATION OF THE PRAYER OF THE MASS

"divine ascension," For he lifted our earthly nature to the divine throne and raised us up with him and made us sit together with the heavenly beings.

"terrible and glorious second coming." Truly terrible and to be feared and glorious and formidable is that coming. For he will come in the glory of the Father and with all the angels and will gather the whole human race for judgment. And he will reward each according to their deeds: giving unspeakable glories to the righteous forever and bitter, eternal punishments to the sinners.

Therefore, we say that we remember all these things and give thanks, offering such a great sacrifice and this holy victim for the benefits received. And through this, we pray to be freed from the future judgment. Therefore, those present cry out:

"We praise you altogether." i.e. we praise you in every way.

"We bless you, we give thanks to you, we implore you, Lord our God." These words, which the assembly says by singing, the priest repeats and explains their meaning by saying:
Indeed, Lord our God, we praise you, we give thanks to you, who have forgiven our sins every day,"
"We praise," he says, "your sweet and gentle and abundant and most merciful forgiveness and give thanks for the abundant gifts of your benefits. For we sin constantly in thoughts, words, deeds, and you do not take revenge on us, but forgive. As if you do not see, you forgive. You not only forgive sins and evil deeds, but also show care and mercy, not only for the body but also for the soul; not a little, but greatly, as demonstrated by the following:
"who have appointed us as ministers of such a terrible and ineffable mystery."

The ineffable holy mystery is said, because words cannot manifest what it is. And it is terrible not only to men, but also to angels. Not because of any good deeds done by us, since we are always found lacking and empty, but relying on your abundant indulgence at all times, we dare to approach the ministry of the body and blood of your Only Begotten. Terrible because we dare to minister not relying on some good deeds we have done, but on your abundant and overflowing kindness at all times. This is what it means: "We dare to approach perpetually to the ministry of the body and blood of your Only Begotten." And why does he always say "ministry" of the sacrament? Because it is not our sacrament to perfect, but we, as the blessed John says, have the order of ministers; he, however, speaks of Christ - who sanctifies and renews. For we offer thanks for the benefits of God by offering at the altar and taking up the ministry. But to unite bread and salvation with oneself is the work of Christ.

Peace to all! Let us adore God. Then the priest says: "We adore and pray and beseech you, Lord, send down upon us and upon these gifts your eternal and consubstantial Holy Spirit."

"We adore and beseech and implore you, Lord." Why does he say: you? He means this: we beseech and adore you, who are the creator and father, who have been kind and beneficent and merciful towards the human race from eternity, who have not only provided creatures for our needs, but have also given us your only begotten and beloved son as our redeemer and vicar. And you place this same son on the altar and feed us with him. Therefore, trusting in your infinite kindness, we beseech you to send the Holy Spirit upon us and upon the sacrifice, so that the Holy Spirit may sanctify us as well.

"who blesses this bread and truly makes it the body of our Lord and redeemer Jesus Christ; and who blesses this cup and truly makes it the blood of our Lord and redeemer Jesus Christ," For the redeemer was made flesh from the Virgin Mary, the Holy Spirit sent by the Father took flesh from the womb of Mary and united it with the divine Word, which was born from her and was manifested as both son and God. The same Holy Spirit acts in the church and on the holy altar. Having united the bread with the Son of God, likewise the cup, and it truly becomes the body and blood of Christ. We see and believe this to happen, because the word of Christ is infallible, who commanded that what he himself first did should be done in his memory until his coming. And confessing the Holy Spirit as coeternal and consubstantial, we profess that he always was with the Father and with the Father himself. Just as the Father was and is and always will be, and there was never a time when he did not exist, so the Holy Spirit is always with the Father and with the Son, and was and is eternal and consubstantial. He also performed this remarkable miracle:

transforming mere bread and wine into the incorruptibility of the body and blood of God.

"So that those who approach may be freed from condemnation, atonement, and forgiveness of sins." In faith, that the Holy Spirit may descend upon the holy sacrifice, we pray according to the Lord's word, professing that it vivifies the body and blood, and with no doubt in mind, we pray. With our minds, we know without doubting or hesitating.

The super sacred altar is the Son of God, accomplishing his own death, which happened for us, as witnesses to us. From this time on, the same body that was on the cross and in the tomb is present. Through him, we seek redemption for the living and the dead. This is the first thing we ask, that we may remain blameless as we administer these terrifying things, and that our approach to him may lead to the remission of sins. That is why he says: "those who approach." For it is unworthy and almost dangerous to stand near and partake in judgment. Therefore, those who are not prepared should not enter, lest they be condemned with a defiled spirit entering the divine chamber. And since no one is found to be immaculate, we ask that sins, whether knowingly or unknowingly committed, be forgiven through the sacrifice of Christ. For those who are conscious of any offense and have not been sanctified by confession and contrition, the prior exhortation has removed them. But even those who have not committed any evil or have repented according to the scriptures should be imbued with fear and trembling. For we are always ensnared by faults: in our thoughts, words, actions, willingly and unwillingly, knowingly and unknowingly. Therefore, they should pray with sighs and fervent tears to be purified from all offenses and to approach in purity and holiness." Through this, grant love, strength, and the desired peace to your holy church," Regarding the sacrifice, he says, "Grant" and not "give," so that we do not say that he repays the good to someone who does good, but rather gives the gift of gratuitous kindness. We pray for "love" to be in the church, that is, among the faithful assemblies: towards God and among themselves; and for "strength" in faith and good works; and for "peace" from external enemies, and that they remain unmoved by the wicked and separated [i.e. heretics]; and that they may altogether enjoy the desirable and beloved peace, as he said, desired."

EXPLANATION OF THE PRAYER OF THE MASS

He goes on to pray for all, from each specific order, saying this: "and to all orthodox bishops," that is, those who are faithful. "To the priests, kings, princes, subjects, travelers, waging wars against barbarians." He prays for mercy for all through the sacrifice of Christ. "Those in distress are those who are in any kind of difficulty. Those waging wars against barbarians" are those who fight wars against foreign and heterodox nations, in order to secure the peace of the Church of Christ. "Through this grant temperate air, abundance of fruits, quick healing for the various pains of the sick laboring in different pains." Temperate air is that which does not harm seeds and plants, but nourishes them well and makes them fruitful. He says that the sick with various pains are those suffering from various types of pain, who, in order to quickly receive healing, whether in body, mind, or soul, he prays. "Through this, grant rest to all who have already passed away in Christ," that is, those who faithfully passed away in Christ from Adam onwards, because not only after the coming, but also before the coming of Christ, those who believed in God passed away in Christ. For He was with God in the beginning, and God was. The saints foresaw Him beforehand. Blessed Gregory the theologian [i.e., Nazianzen] speaks of the perfected ones. But the imperfect ones professing Him as God, whom the prophets and the righteous preached, worshiped the holy Trinity, even if they were unaware of the distinction of persons. Therefore, they too are called those who passed away in Christ. Therefore, when he says: grant rest to those who have passed away in Christ," he refers not only to the recently deceased, but also to the holy fathers who passed away from Adam to Abraham and from him onwards.

"prophets, apostles, martyrs, bishops, priests, deacons, and all the clergy of your holy Church," that is, subdeacons, scribes, readers, and psalmists. The word "all" indicates everyone who is in the ecclesiastical order, which is called the clergy of the Church. For all are dedicated to the ministry and service of the holy Church.
"and of the lay state, to the men who have believed in Christ and to the women."

Now he commemorates all faithful laypeople, both those of old and those who have recently passed away in faith. Just as we say that the prayers and intercessions of the saints are helpful to us, so too we must assist the deceased with prayers, especially through the holy Mass, which is the hope, life, and redemption of the departed. For we can mention by name the deceased loved ones and acquaintances. of

EXPLANATION OF THE PRAYER OF THE MASS

others, we ask God to remember them, who knows all. Therefore, we remember each of the orders of the saints, and we join all the faithful as if they were one body of Christ, whose common head is the commemoration of Christ's sacrifice before God the Father. And so we bring this prayer to its conclusion.

"We also, with these, keep, bless, and love, O Lord!" He says: with all those we have mentioned, may you also keep us, that is, seek us out, be our protector, for both yours and ours. The deacon repeats the same as the priest mentions, speaking each chapter loudly at intervals. And for each chapter, the assembly present at the mystery says clearly with a loud voice: "Remember, Lord, and have mercy!"

This exhortation includes many chapters in itself: first of the Mother of God, then of various saints according to their order: patriarchs, prophets, apostles, bishops, martyrs, priests, deacons, chosen women, female martyrs, holy kings, holy princes, holy doctors, holy fathers, and martyrs, superiors, all hermits, and others who in any way have been accepted by God. For in each order, some are mentioned by name from the entire order.
those others who are of the same order are added. They command those who take care of good discipline during the Easter festival. Those who are to be mentioned briefly during the sacred time of the Mass are:

"The commemoration of the Virgin Mary, John the Baptist, and Saint Stephen shall be made. Let there be a commemoration of the holy Apostles, prophets, martyrs, the Fathers, Paul, and all the saints. Let there be a commemoration of the holy patriarchs, orthodox bishops, priests, and all the clergy of the Church. Let there be a commemoration of faithful men and women who have died in Christ."

I will strive to explain what these commemorations mean, with my limited understanding. Giving thanks to God for many and varied favors, we offer the holy sacrifice of Christ's offering, by which we commemorate all the benefits of God and give thanks for all. And above all, we give thanks for His chosen ones in the holy mystery. Because we are all one in Christ, the glorification of our brethren is our glory. Offering the great sacrifice, we commemorate the action of thanksgiving for them towards Him who made them so good and excellent, and victorious in all the battles against the devil. We give thanks not only for the saints, but also for all who have been deemed worthy to believe in God. Solomon said: "To know God is all justice." And to be His people and the offspring of holy baptism and to be a partaker of holy communion, and to be reborn in the holy name of Christ through death, the great glory. And they offer thanks to all of these and similar things by means of the holy sacrifice, those who have received gifts. With this sacrifice, we not only give thanks to God for each of the saints, but we also supplicate, remembering the strength and excellent life of the saints. We give thanks for the holy sacrifice and supplicate, as we have Christ's death and the saints' mortifications interceding with the heavenly Father for all the faithful, living and deceased. For we, rejoicing with the saints, offer to God their offerings and thanksgivings, imputing their crowns to us, and they are like protectors of their members interceding with God, especially during the time of the awe-inspiring sacrifice. And we, giving thanks through them, when each chapter is recited, say: "Remember, Lord, and have mercy!" i.e., remember the love and labor of the saints towards you, and have mercy on us, because they are ours and from us. And we are all one church and of one Christ, who is our head, we are all body and members. Therefore, as we commemorate the saints, we begin again to ask for mercy through the holy sacrifice, enumerating each order, with these words: "Remember, Lord, and have mercy and bless your holy Zion, the Catholic, apostolic church, which you redeemed with the precious blood of your only begotten and freed, and grant it your infinite peace." Zion is: mother, in our language. And it is fitting that prayers be for the Jerusalemite church, because of the sacred places that are in Jerusalem. For that church was first founded, and then all the churches of the world. And if it calls the whole church mother Zion, this is not difficult to understand. For the holy church gives birth to us by sacred baptism and feeds us with spiritual food. "Catholic" means universal. We ask for mercy for all the churches, which were founded throughout the world by the preaching of the apostles, therefore we call them "apostolic." But those who have strayed from the profession of the apostles' faith are not called apostolic. Apostolic.

However, even though the churches are in many places, yet one is professed for the unity of faith. For this reason, as if from one, the he church is called: "whom you have redeemed with the precious blood of your only begotten and freed." For by the sacred blood of Christ, we are redeemed from curses and sins and death, and freed from the servitude of Satan. Therefore, it does not mention the names of many churches, but the church, and not: which, but: whom you have redeemed. Nor does it say: give them, but: give it your unmoving peace.

"Remember, O Lord, and have mercy and bless all orthodox bishops, who, living justly, preach the word of truth correctly."

What is "to preach correctly"? This is a completely right and true doctrine, to which no perversion or corruption is added, neither to the right nor to the left. That is why it adds: "the word of truth." For truth is one, lies are divided into many. Concerning this word "hamarot" (brief) Isaiah had prophesied before, and Paul explains: "The word will be finished and cut short in righteousness, the Lord will make a short word on the earth." Which is not multiform like laws. But by believing in the Holy Trinity and in the incarnation of Christ, we are justified. Therefore, we pray through the mercy of God, that bishops who preach correctly may be strengthened for the labors of their office. We pray in general for all, but especially for him whom we have as our leader, saying this:

"And especially for our teacher and overseer and guardian of our souls, Bishop N. N., whom you, O Lord, give to us for many days!"

Why was it not enough to say only "bishop," but added: our teacher and overseer and guardian of our souls? So that with a fervent heart and sincere love, we may pray for him. We know better than the bishop what should be asked; namely, that he should be diligent in teaching, administer the oversight firmly, and that all souls, whether such and such, may not be lazy in good works or have any blemish. I will have a label in my soul, observe the new sluggishness, not helping them with prayers and admonitions, guarding with all vigilance, seeking the profit of the flock rather than his own. And knowing this, we pray diligently for our bishops. For considering this also: we must compensate for their prayers for us with our own prayers for them. For especially then, those prayers that are sent out for us by them are heard by God, if we pray for them. In this way, Paul admonishes the Corinthians: "Our mouth is open to you, our heart is wide. You are not restricted by us," that is, even though there are many of you, and there are other souls for us, our spirit is not restricted to forget or neglect anyone in admonition and prayers. "But you," he says, "are restricted in your affections." You do not care for me alone as much as I care for you and all. And he adds here: "I have the same reward as for little children; be enlarged as well." In order to help them again, he said this. He could not provide help for himself, as he himself said, but for many. Therefore, in all his letters, he commands prayers to be made for him. Taking care of their assistance more than his own, he used their prayers. But he wanted them to be helped by themselves as much as he was helped by them. Therefore, when he spoke about prayers, he did not say, "for my benefit," but "for the abundance of words for the redemption of men."

"Remember, Lord, and have mercy and bless us and your people who are present, and me who celebrates the Mass, and grant to each what is useful and beneficial."

"Saying to us, he signifies those who are present before the sacrament. And the people" indicates the entire assembly. "The one celebrating Mass is named the one who administers the sacrament. "And grant to each what is useful and beneficial." We often ask for harmful things, but you, who know what is useful and beneficial for us, grant for the health of each, that is, for the health of all of us as a father and creator.

"Remember, Lord, and have mercy and bless those." They offer gifts to your holy church, to those who mercifully remember the poor; and reward what they agree to in their prayers, according to your innate riches: a hundredfold, here and there." Some offer vessels of offerings to the church, others sacred books, donate fruits from the field, from the winepress, from the animals. And not only on the feast days of the Redeemer and the memorials of the saints do they offer according to their abilities. And we pray for these and for the merciful, who receive the poor from their own resources. He did not add "mercifully" lightly, but so that we may remember to recall the poor with compassion and mercy and with more zeal for God's pleasure than for gifts. Which the apostle also says: "Mercy depends on the will, and to act depends on the ability. But they consider such a debtor to God." We ask that he may repay according to his innate riches. "Innate" means: according to his own nature. That is: the nature of your essence is mercy. Repay a hundredfold here: for one hundred, and there: with ineffable deposits. Remember, Lord, and have mercy and bless the souls of the departed." We ask as if he would remember them in his kingdom, as he remembered the thief, and bless them mercifully with those on his right who hear the voice of the blessed: Come, you blessed of my

EXPLANATION OF THE PRAYER OF THE MASS

Father, inherit the kingdom prepared for you." Remember, Lord, also those who have entrusted themselves to our prayers, and direct the plans of the prayers they make and we, to the right end and to the fullness of redemption." Just as a charioteer guides the animals and does not allow them to stray from the road, so may you be the guide of our prayers, may they not deviate from your will, whether something earthly is sought or the evil vengeance of enemies, or mountains are removed from the understanding of prayers and swayed here and there. But let the mind be lifted up to heaven, and let useful and salutary things be sought from God with a holy mind, and let them fill all our redemption. "And reward all" i.e. give reward to all. With what? "With immortal and blessed happiness." i.e. that which does not pass away and blesses those who receive it. "Cleanse our thoughts" purifying them from the anguish of conscience and evil deeds.

And make us temples, so that we may receive the body and blood of your only begotten Lord and Redeemer Jesus Christ, prepare dwellings and homes for us, he says, of your only begotten with this saving sacrifice. "With whom, Almighty Father," that is, with your Son, Almighty Father, "along with the life-giving and liberating Holy Spirit belongs glory, principality, honor, now and always, and unto the ages of ages. Amen."

Exhortation

"To you, Almighty Father, we offer thanksgiving and glorification for the holy, immortal, divine sacrifice that is upon the sacred altar."

The Father is the only begotten Son and Lord of all. As God, He is almighty. We offer thanksgiving and words of glorification, he says, because He has made us worthy to place such a sacrifice on the fearful altar, not taken from the earth, from animals, but from heaven, divine. For the Son of God is the sacrifice, immaculate, whole, which He calls holy. And although it appears as a sign of death, it is life-giving. Therefore, He calls it "immortal." Just as Christ's body, when He laid down His human soul, was alive, because it was God's body, united with God, made one by mixture, and when He wished to rise, He raised Himself - so the same life of divinity, united with the bread and the cup, is immortal and gives immortality to those who partake. Just as that body, dying, brought many from death to life, so, while the sacrifice is a memorial of the Lord's death, it vivifies those cleansed from the anguish of conscience who partake of it. For they rose who were vivified by Christ's death. And see now the cross at this hour and believe: He is present now, for this is not inferior to that body, but it is the same, and indeed it is that. Therefore the Lord promised eternal life to those who partake of this. But just as no one was ever made alive from the impious, so now no one who is not holy, no one unrepentant, finds life. If indeed they were ever insolent, like Judas, they would be condemned like him. And after making thanksgiving for such great gifts, he prays with these words: "Grant us these gifts for redemption and life."

And according to the one who is above the altar, the Mass makes us conform. "Through this, grant charity, steadfastness, the longed-for peace to your holy Church and to all orthodox bishops; to our archbishop and to the priest celebrating Mass." Although the priest has already prayed, the deacon repeats the prayer in a loud voice, so that all may hear and all may sing together with one voice, and so that we may be taught that prayers for our leaders are no less necessary than gifts of charity towards God and among ourselves, of steadfastness and peace.

"For this reason, Lord, remember those who celebrate according to your unfailing mercy." Since God the creator is merciful towards all creatures, he implores that those who celebrate do not forget the Creator's mercy, but remember it and take care of it.

"Remember, Lord, the souls of the departed who hoped in you." Because we are commanded to pray for those who have passed away in faith and hope, he says this so that he may remember the souls of the departed who hoped in him.

"By your power, Lord, and by this immortal sacrifice, give us life and have mercy on us." Because, he says, this sacrifice is for us, therefore, through the holy sacrifice that gives life, he says, may your power have mercy on us.

Prayers
"God of truth, and father of mercy,"
You are God by nature, he says, for you are the creator; but you have become a father through mercy. Therefore, he says that he is God: "of truth."

EXPLANATION OF THE PRAYER OF THE MASS

"Father, that is truly; and Father: 'mercy, that is: oh, clemency. We give thanks to you, who honored our sinful nature more than the blessed patriarchs. For whereas God was called Father by them, you willed to be called Father by us."

God says: "I am the God of Abraham, Isaac, Jacob. And he said that his faithful are his children. Therefore, Christ commanded us to call God our Father when praying. And the apostle said: "You are no longer a servant, but a son." Therefore, he gives thanks for the infinite kindness. For more mercifully than the saints [i.e. patriarchs], you honored our sinful condemned nature. God, And now, may you make your great, new, and precious grace of this name shine forth daily and flourish in your church."

For by this grace you have made our nature worthy to be called sons and to be called Father by us, never forgetting to have mercy on us as a father, even if we have sinned, and not to cast us out of this most honorable grace, but as with burning clemency, you have bestowed upon us the new and precious grace of that name, so may you preserve it shining forth and flourishing daily in your church, that is, in your faithful.

And grant us to open our mouths with a free voice and call upon you, Heavenly Father, and say: "Grant us the grace of your mercy that we may boldly seek refuge in your clemency and piety and infinite indulgence and call upon you, the earthly and heavenly Father of sinners, who are holy and celestial. He did not add this: "that we may open our mouths," but because our mouths are constantly closed by the sins of our lips, for which reason we pray that he may purify and sanctify our mouths and give us the confidence to open our mouths and call upon the Father freely.

The prayer "Our Father who art in heaven" was more fully explained by Saint Gregory of Nyssa and Saint John Chrysostom. Therefore, those who wish may be more accurately instructed. "Our Father, who art in heaven." For according to the flesh we have earthly fathers, but in baptism we are born through the Holy Spirit and made participants in the Father of Christ by His body and blood, we have a heavenly Father, the Father, the progenitor of Christ, with whom we are united. Therefore, the Lord taught us to say: "Our Father, who art in heaven, hallowed be thy name, let your name be holy and glorious to us. Thy

EXPLANATION OF THE PRAYER OF THE MASS

kingdom come, the kingdom is the name of the empire. We pray that the new grace of Christ may govern us, so that our sins do not rule over us and lead us into the servitude of Satan. We long for the coming of His future empire, where Satan and the dominion of sins are overthrown. Thy will be done, as in heaven, so on earth. Just as in heaven there is no perversion or sin, but everything is done according to your will, so may sedition be removed from the earth and men be made angelic, so that all may become doers of your will. Give us this day our daily bread, give us the necessary sustenance for our bodies each day. And forgive us our debts, whatever we have sinned and whatever offense we have committed, for which we are worthy of punishment, forgive us. As we forgive our debtors, i.e. those who have wronged us. And lead us not into temptation, whether Satan tempts or men: through sins or dangers. But deliver us from evil, from all the snares of Satan. Lord of lords, God of gods, the God and Lord of all lords and gods. You are the God of angels and priests. Heavenly Father, we beseech you, do not lead us into temptation or condemnation, but deliver us from evil, save us from temptation. Be our liberator from temptation in a paternal manner. Keep us blameless and deliver us from evil, for you are powerful. Altogether, and victorious above all is your dominion, therefore he added here: "Yours is the power and the empire. And glory befits you, principality, honor, now and always and into eternity of eternities."

Prayers

"You who are the source of life and the head of mercy," Life and mercy proceed from you, as from a fountain.
"Have mercy on this assembly, which bows down to worship your divinity." May your assembly delight in this perpetual fountain, which worships your divinity. And over those who bow down before you: "preserve them safe."

"Safe" is the same as "healthy" as we call it. Let all present, he says, be preserved safe.

"Impress on their souls the form of the body's appearance", For just as with our bodily eyes the mystery is shown having a bodily form, so also in our souls may the trembling of the mystery of divine glory be depicted. For the impression is the form of the appearance. Therefore, just as the apostle says we see his glory as if in a mirror, we pray that we may see the invisible glory of the sacrifice.

EXPLANATION OF THE PRAYER OF THE MASS

"For the inheritance and portion of future goods", "We are called by lot," says the apostle, "predestined." Also, we pray that no one may be found rejected, but alet us be heirs of future goods and share them with Him. He also adds: "through Jesus Christ, our Lord," By His grace, may they be made worthy of future goods, of which they have received a pledge through Jesus Christ our Lord. "With whom, to you, Holy Spirit and Father almighty, befitting glory, principality, honor; now and always and unto the ages of ages. Amen."

Holy Father, who called us Christians in the name of your only begotten Son, the things that are done because of the offering of the sacrifice are completed: thanksgivings and prayers, and with this concluded, special blessings of the Holy Trinity and with a repeated blessing and glory, the thanksgiving and prayers begin again, not for all of humanity, but only for the faithful. And because he said with a loud voice that holiness befits the saints, he also revealed what kind of holiness they are, saying: Holy Father, Holy Son, Holy Spirit; and the holy sacrifice of Christ, he says, as an offering fitting to the Holy Trinity. And those who wish to partake in the holiness, he says, must themselves be pure and holy. And since human nature is always contaminated by sins and cannot be without sin altogether, for the help of our lowliness, the mercy of God is called upon, through which having attained purity, we may approach the pure. - And first saying: "Father," he moves the mercy of the merciful God, no less than what he says afterwards to the Father: Who called us Christians in the name of your only begotten Son. For you have given us such grace, he says, that we receive the name of your only begotten Son. For he is named Christ, but we are Christians, that is, those who belong to Christ. Through him we give thanks and show devotion. For if, while we were strangers, you were compelled by your love to show mercy to us to the extent that you made us the possession and heirs of your only begotten Son.

We have received the name from You, and now, as we are Christians, You show us great mercy, because Your only begotten and beloved Son is ours and we are named by Him. "And You have given us spiritual baptism through the washing for the remission of sins," You have not only given us possession and inheritance according to Your promise through the prophet to Your only Son: "I will give you the nations as your inheritance," but You also wanted to make us brothers of Your beloved and consubstantial Son, so that He may be the firstborn among many brothers. Therefore, You cleansed the mud of our sins by the washing of baptism. And by the second birth through the Holy Spirit, You have raised us up to be sons. Through Him, the ardor of paternal love seeks to warm us. For the Holy Spirit, who proceeds from You and has made us heavenly, and in order for us to be adopted sons, has lifted us up to make us worthy to partake in the body and blood of Your only begotten Son. For Your love towards us has grown to the point that You did not bear to have Your Son on one side and us, whom You have adopted by grace, on the other side. But You desired to mix Him with us out of love for mankind, so that He Himself may become our head, and we may be His body and members, and be one in body and blood with Christ, united and joined to Him.

As the apostle says: "we are many, yet one body in Christ, and therefore we are all one Son." Therefore, with the remembrance of such ineffable love, prayers are offered, so that we may not be deprived of honor and grace because of the guilt of our sins. But from such great offenses, lead us to such great goodness, purify us now, and make us approach as such to the body and blood of Christ. Then he says: "make us now worthy to receive this communion for the remission of sins," He says communion, because He is united with us, and we with Him. For such great grace, it is fitting to give thanks. And so he says: "and in all things, let us continually glorify the Father and Son and Holy Spirit, now and always and unto ages of ages.

"Of the holy, precious body and blood of our Lord and Redeemer Jesus Christ, which is distributed among us [we shall eat]. This is life, the hope of resurrection, expiation, the forgiveness of our sins." He turns to the convent, to which they should approach and with whom they should communicate, advising: To the Holy of Holies, to Him who is more precious than all the earth and every creature, to the creator of all, to the maker of all precious things. - He says, "This is the body and blood of our Lord and Redeemer to which we approach. He is our Lord and Redeemer: Jesus Christ. He redeemed us from Satan, freed us from the bondage of our sins, and gained power over us. - - He, crucified for us with unbroken bones, remained on the cross. But now He is divided and distributed among us, so that we may be united with all. This is life. For our Lord said, "Whoever eats this bread will live forever." - And it is the hope of resurrection. For our Lord also said, "I will raise up on the last day those who eat from this bread." He did not say: those who do not eat from this bread will not rise, but they will rise not to life, but to judgment, which is why their resurrection is not honorable, but a punishment. For our Lord said: "To those who have done good, the resurrection of life, and to those who have done evil, the resurrection of judgment." Therefore, those who become participants of His body truly rise. And the priest takes up this hope, saying to the convent: "This is life, the hope of resurrection." But also "expiation," he says, "and the forgiveness of our sins." For after baptism, sins are purged by approaching the lamb with confession and penitence. For the purification of baptism purifies in the manner of a bath, and the communion of the sacrament is like a furnace... For in baptism, we are immersed in the waters of purification; there we are transformed into the nature of gold and silver, which no longer needs cleansing but requires a furnace. Therefore, one who enters this terrible fire is purified. And just as there is a need to purify gold and silver, so also is there a need for others.

With some materials, as afterwards they are cleansed by fire from impurity, so here too confession and penance together are effective for purification. And just as there it burns only by itself.

The fire does not melt nor distinguish gold and silver from clay, so too when one approaches the spiritual fire without confession and penitence, you may be burned and not truly sanctified. But when you approach with penitence: it is the sanctification of the mind. The gift [of Holy Communion] in so many ways helps when you hear the assembly of priests speaking, all these things testify saying: Amen."

Sing a psalm to our God!
Sing a psalm to the beneficent and heavenly king, who sits upon the Cherubim!
Sing a psalm and give glory to the Father and the Son and the Holy Spirit, now and forever and unto the ages of ages!"

Although He is seen on the altar, yet He is in heaven and among the Cherubim: the God and king of all. Therefore: Sing a psalm and give glory to Him and with the Father and the Holy Spirit. For God and king who sits upon the Cherubim, places Himself on the altar as food and drink for us. And may the holy Trinity be glorified, now and forever and unto the ages of ages.

Which the deacon repeats and mixes with other things, saying:

"Sing a psalm to the Lord our God, choir, with sweet voice! For psalms and spiritual songs are fitting to Him."

It is fitting to sing a psalm to Him who loved us so much with a sweet voice. Sweet is the blessing that comes from a holy mind with sincere love to God. "And especially those of you who have received from the holy, immortal, incorruptible, divine sacrament, give thanks to the Lord!" For we have been taught by the Lord. He gave thanks before instituting the sacrament, so that we may also do the same.

Therefore, the deacon encourages and commands to give thanks: "And especially those of you who have received" etc. He says: give thanks, when you have received in faith the body and blood of God. This is indicated by saying: "from the holy, immortal, incorruptible, divine sacrament." For God is wholly holy and without death and corruption. Therefore the apostle says: "Who alone possesses immortality." Others do not possess immortality and incorruptibility by their own nature, but receive it from Him. "Give thanks"

Stir yourselves, because through the holy you are sanctified, and through the immortal you attain immortality and progress towards God to be deified. Then the assembly speaks with one voice: "We give thanks to you, Lord."

"We give thanks to you, Christ, our redeemer, who have granted us the banquet of such great goodness for the salvation of life." First, because he saved us, thanks are given, and then, because he gave such a banquet, in which salvation is granted and life. For all the cunning of demons is kept away, if they see in us the communion of the saving sacrament, as the blessed teacher John says: The devil sees the terrible fire bursting forth from our mouths when we are refreshed by the sacrament; and therefore, he cannot approach to do harm, but flees far away, and we are saved. We are preserved through this [i.e. through the holy communion] even from future wrath. We are enlivened here by righteousness, because we receive strength for every work of righteousness. For just as those who are deprived of righteousness are dead to the grace of God, they only live in sins, acting impiously with all their members, so those who worthily receive the holy sacrament are filled with the grace of God, they die to sins with all their members, and they live with all their [members] in righteousness. For their eyes are always turned towards God according to the scriptures, they attend to God and those things that are of God. With their ears they listen to divine admonitions. Their mouth speaks spiritual wisdom, their tongue speaks of righteousness. With the precepts of God fixed in their minds, they constantly hold to the firm path [i.e. of communion], they enrich their hands for the work of the Lord at all times, they remind that their hands should be raised to God, and they keep them in the habit of prayer. Such a way of living in this world is given by communion and there is the infinite and eternal life which is of Christ and with Christ.

And with the giving of thanks for these things, the prayer begins: "Preserve us holy and immaculate with this [banquet]." Do not allow evil, it says, to find a place to dwell in us, to defile and pollute us. But be with us and keep us holy and blameless. Therefore, he adds here: "and dwelling within us, feed us with your divine care in the field of your holy will and the goodness of a loving God." For you are such a merciful shepherd that you nourish the sheep from your own members, may the same mercy dwell within us and guard us from the wolf and lead us far from deadly pastures. And where this is, the following indicate: "feed us in the field of your holy will and the goodness of a loving God."

For the will of Christ is righteousness and good works, by which, he says, we are made worthy. This is the green field, of which the psalmist sings. This is the field, which is according to the will of Christ, inaccessible to the wolf, a city fortified with the castle of the law, as it says: "in which we are protected from all devilish infestation." The devil's infestation is to oppose good with evil: pride to humility, anger to meekness, envy to charity, greed to modesty, weakness to strength, and so on, opposing vices to other virtues. From these, he says, we are protected. "May we become worthy to listen to your voice alone and to follow you, the victor and true shepherd."

He prays that we may hear according to the word of the Lord: "My sheep hear my voice, and I know them, and they follow me, and I give them eternal life." They ask for the same words of prayer, that we may hear his teaching voice and follow him. - And this is to follow: to deny oneself, to always walk with the cross in mind, to go the same path that the Lord showed, to bear hardships and troubles in life, to receive there what he demands in the following words: "and from you we may receive a place prepared in your kingdom." According to each one's dignity, places are prepared in the kingdom of Christ, when he extinguishes kingdoms and only his kingdom stands and remains forever. These dwelling places ask for the words of prayer and add here the reasons for the beneficence: "Our God and our Lord, Jesus Christ," For you are the Creator, he says, and the Lord, who has freed us from sins and made us worthy to partake in your dominion.

Through your sufferings, we have received incorruption. Not only do you rule over us as the Creator, as you do over other creatures, but because you have purchased us with a precious price, giving us your life-giving blood. Therefore, in glorifying, he concludes his speech saying:

"To whom belong glory, dominion, honor; now and forever and ever."
"Peace to all."
"The inscrutable, inaccessible, triune essence, the firm foundation, the receiver, inseparably consubstantial Holy Trinity."

"Inscrutable" is said because it does not undergo, not in the least, examination. 'Inaccessible': because even if someone presumes to approach, they cannot comprehend the substance or eternity of God. 'Triune': according to personality. For the Father is and the Son and the Holy Spirit; distinct in persons, united in divinity. 'Essence' is, because it does not receive existence from anyone, but is in itself, as the holy Illuminator says: The Lord God, who is the sole essence; nor is there anyone before Him." 'Firm foundation' is, because it established creatures created out of nothing and maintains them firm in their respective order. 'Receiver' is, because it receives and has compassion on all things made through itself and prepares what is necessary for everyone, not only for angels and humans, but for all living beings. And it gives form and place to each one. It preserves the lofty and splendid courses of the stars. It holds the earth immovable, and adorns it with various germs, plants, and seeds, which it irrigates with rain clouds until they are satisfied. But it also confines the sea within its boundaries, so that it does not engulf the lands or spread beyond its limits, beyond measure. 'Inseparable is the Holy Trinity, because, although the Holy Trinity is divided by personality, yet according to divinity, it is indivisible. There is one nature in the Holy Trinity, one essence, one dominion, one will, one glory. And to her alone belongs the worship of all that exists, as he says to those who follow: "To whom belong glory, dominion, honor; now and forever and ever."

EXPLANATION OF THE PRAYER OF THE MASS

Monita

By the grace of God, we have brought to completion an explanation of the rituals of the Church that have been instituted for each season. We have not elaborated on the sentiments of exhortations and the words of prayers, but to the extent of our understanding, we have briefly explained. Indeed, there is a great variety of ecclesiastical rituals, exhortations, prayers, and Masses; there are rituals that are established in memory of martyrs, those for the feast of the Lord's birth, resurrection, and for obtaining graces, such as in baptism, in the laying on of hands [i.e. in ordination], in the blessing of the crown [i.e. in marriage], in the burial of the deceased, in the consecration of the altar, in the blessing of church vessels, in the hallowing of water on the feast of the Epiphany of the Lord, in the blessing of the cross, in the blessing of seeds, fields, calves, salt, grains, and other sacred administrations, and those rituals for travelers, the sick, and others like them: if we were to discuss all of these word for word, not only would we not be equal to the task in writing, but even the readers would not be able to listen. But if one attentively focuses on what has been said, one will understand everything else. But what do we mean by what we have written, that it opens the way to understanding all that we have left unsaid? If one part of these things, which is only partially understood, suffices for the performance of all ecclesiastical rituals.

Therefore, I ask that you do not consider the contemplation of divine words, especially exhortations and prayers, to be empty work. For our salvation, and not only ours but also that of those to whom we owe benefits, whether living or dead, depends on these. Nor does a word that sounds harsh help anything unless the mind follows it. For God, who sees into the minds, looks at the hearts and minds, not just the mouths. Therefore, with a vigilant spirit, tranquil thought, and attentive mind, let us offer prayers to God, that we may help ourselves and others, and benefit from the prayers of others. For if we pray with our whole heart for all the faithful, we will receive help through the prayers of all the faithful. "For with what measure you measure, it shall be measured to you." Because of myself first and then all others, I attend, so that we may take care of ourselves and ask for God's help, so according to God's good pleasure we may be able to offer our prayers to Him. And especially the leaders of the church should pay attention, who lift their hands to God for the whole church, and reconcile all supplications to God.

Those who have confidence in speaking to God should adopt their manners; so that, like Moses, they may be worthy to see God within the mountains, and have the holy departed as visible helpers of prayers and through them perform the commands of the people before God. And if I said they should become like Moses, let no one think this is absurd. For the apostles who gave us the presbytery represented Aaron and Moses to us. And they ordered us to enter such a ministry. And if we do not obey those laws anymore, this happens: partly because we are convinced by the word of God about this matter, partly because [if we were to obey the laws] we would seek our own interests, not Christ's. For Christ, who followed the laws, did not consider them worthy to enter the kingdom. Nor did he warn only the priests about this matter, but everyone together. For he began to speak to the gathered multitude of men and women who had approached at that time, so that it would be evident to all who would believe afterwards that he established this rule. And what did he say? Unless your righteousness exceeds that of the scribes and Pharisees, you will not enter the kingdom of heaven." And if he says this to everyone, how much more does he demand abundance from the priests? And rightfully so: For those who were priests according to the law performed the priestly office through the blood of animals. For they were ministering shadows, whom Paul says have served as examples and figures of heavenly things. But those who have become priests of grace and truth are appointed to administer the blood of the Son of God. And this is what Paul called "heavenly," and of which he says that everything of old was its example and figure. For although it is accomplished on earth [i.e. in the Holy Mass], yet not with earthly offerings, but with that bread coming down from heaven and giving life to the world.

Therefore, the blessed Paul, mentioning the figurative sacrifices, again says: "Therefore it was necessary for the examples to such gifts", but it is appropriate for heavenly sacrifices to be better than those [i.e., purify]." Do you see that he not only calls the sacrifice heavenly, but also us, who share in the heavenly sacrifice? This is further shown elsewhere, when he says: "Holy brothers, participants in the heavenly calling." Indeed, we offer a heavenly sacrifice. Therefore, it follows that there should be much greater abundance for us than for those who in ancient times were ministers of shadows. "For," the Lord says, "from him to whom much is given, much will be required." Therefore, let us take on perfect virtues, so that we may be perfect. Let us save ourselves and many others. And may the Lord Christ be a common helper to all in any matter, and may His holy name be glorified among us, to whom be glory forever. Amen.

EXPLANATION OF THE PRAYER OF THE MASS

The Scriptorium Project is the work of a small group of lay people of various apostolic churches who are interested in the preservation, transmission, and translation of the works of the early and medieval church. Our efforts are to make the works of the church fathers accessible to anyone who might have an interest in Christian antiquities and the theological, philosophical, and moral writings that have become the bedrock of Western Civilization.

To-date, our releases have pulled from the Greek, Syriac, Georgian, Latin, Celtic, Ethiopian, and Coptic traditions of Christianity, and have been pulled from sundry local traditions and languages.

www.ingramcontent.com/pod-product-compliance
Lightning Source LLC
LaVergne TN
LVHW052004060526
838201LV00059B/3836